A Guide for Using

Sounder

in the Classroom

Based on the novel written by William H. Armstrong

This guide written by Mari Lu Robbins

Teacher Created Resources, Inc.
6421 Industry Way
Westminster, CA 92683
www.teachercreated.com
©*1994 Teacher Created Resources, Inc.*
Reprinted, 2005
Made in U.S.A.
ISBN 1-55734-530-9

Teacher Created Resources

Edited by
Janet Cain.

Illustrated by
Kris Sexton

Cover Art by
Nancee McClure

Table of Contents

Introduction

A good book can touch our lives in many ways. It can transport us to another place and time, introduce us to different characters, touch our hearts, and inspire us to accomplish our goals. Each time we reread it, we are able to recapture some of our original experience while discovering new things that make it even more special.

In *Literature Units*, great care has been taken to select books which are sure to touch your students' lives.

Teachers who use this unit will find the following features to supplement their own valuable ideas.

- Sample Lesson Plans

- Pre-reading Activities

- A Biographical Sketch and Picture of the Author

- A Book Summary

- Vocabulary Lists and Suggested Vocabulary Activities

- Chapters grouped for study with the sections including:

    — *quizzes*

    — *hands-on projects*

    — *cooperative learning activities*

    — *cross-curriculum connections*

    — *extensions into the reader's own life*

- Post-reading Activities

- Book Report Ideas

- Research Ideas

- A Culminating Activity

- Three Different Options for Unit Tests

- A Bibliography

- An Answer Key

We are confident that this unit will be a valuable addition to your planning and hope that as you use our ideas your students will find reading to be a more fulfilling experience.

Sample Lesson Plan

Each of the lessons suggested below can take from one to several days to complete.

LESSON 1
- Introduce and complete some or all of the pre-reading activities found on page 5.
- Read "About the Author" with your students. (page 6)
- Introduce the vocabulary list for Section 1. (page 8)

LESSON 2
- Read the Author's Note and Chapter I. As you read, place the vocabulary words in the context of the story and discuss their meanings.
- Choose a vocabulary activity. (page 9)
- Make a shadow puppet of Sounder. (page 11)
- Compare opinions before and after reading the story. (page 12)
- Make a mini-book of African-American history. (page 13)
- Begin "Reading Response Journals." (page 14)
- Administer the Section 1 quiz. (page 10)
- Introduce the vocabulary list for Section 2. (page 8)

LESSON 3
- Read Chapters II and III. Place the vocabulary words in context and discuss their meanings.
- Choose a vocabulary activity. (page 9)
- Make a crossword puzzle using information from the story. (page 16)
- Be a detective and learn to differentiate between fingerprints. (page 17)
- Create riddles for others to solve. (page 18)
- Examine what life was like before and after a catastrophic event. (page 19)
- Administer the Section 2 quiz. (page 15)
- Introduce the vocabulary list for Section 3. (page 8)

LESSON 4
- Read Chapters IV and V. Place the vocabulary words in context and discuss their meanings.
- Choose a vocabulary activity. (page 9)
- Bake a cake. (page 21)
- Conduct a mock trial. (page 22)
- Summarize the first ten amendments to the Bill of Rights and explain their importance. (page 23)
- Write lyrics to a song. (page 24)

- Administer the Section 3 quiz. (page 20)
- Introduce the vocabulary list for Section 4. (page 8)

LESSON 5
- Read Chapters VI and VII. Place the vocabulary words in context and discuss their meanings.
- Choose a vocabulary activity. (page 9)
- Make a diorama of a schoolhouse. (page 26)
- Present a skit of a scene from the story. (page 27)
- Write a newspaper article. (page 28)
- Tell about strategies for coping with stressful situations. (page 29)
- Administer the Section 4 quiz. (page 25)
- Introduce the vocabulary words for Section 5. (page 8)

LESSON 6
- Read Chapter VIII. Place the vocabulary words in context and discuss their meanings.
- Make a board game using information from the story. (page 31)
- Examine prejudice. (page 32)
- Locate places and geographic features on a map of Georgia. (page 33)
- Write a letter to the author. (page 34).
- Administer the Section 5 quiz. (page 30)

LESSON 7
- Discuss any questions your students may have about the story. (page 35)
- Assign book reports and research projects. (pages 36 and 37)
- Begin work on a culminating activity. (pages 38, 39, 40, and 41)

LESSON 8
- Administer unit tests 1,2, and/or 3. (pages 42, 43, and 44)
- Discuss the test answers and possibilities.
- Discuss the students' enjoyment of the book.
- Provide a list of related reading for your students. (page 45)

Before the Book

Before you begin reading *Sounder*, do some pre-reading activities with your students to stimulate their interest, enhance their comprehension, and help them gain an understanding of the time period and cultural framework in which the book is set. Here are some activities that might work well in your class.

1. Predict what the story might be about by hearing the title and looking at the cover illustration.

2. Discuss what the story might be about after reading the "Author's Note" at the beginning of the book.

3. Discuss other books written by William H. Armstrong that students may have heard about or read.

4. Answer these questions.

   •   Are you interested in:

       — stories that take place after the Civil War?

       — stories about growing up?

       — stories that reveal instances of cruelty and injustice?

       — stories about a special pet?

       — stories that are emotionally moving?

       — stories about people who become stronger as a result of adversity?

   •   Would you ever:

       — treat persons badly because of their race?

       — steal food for your family?

       — walk for miles to go to school?

       — want to change historical events?

5. Describe a situation in which you or someone you know experienced prejudice.

6. Discuss historical fiction.

7. Discuss the issue of slavery in America. Why was slave labor used? How might it have affected the attitudes of some people toward African Americans? How did it make African Americans feel about themselves? When and why did slavery end?

About the Author

William H. Armstrong was born September 14, 1914, in Lexington, Virginia, to Howard Gratton and Ida (Morris) Armstrong. His writing career got off to a rather shaky start. In high school, he had an assignment to write an original story. He chose to write about what went on inside the mind of a physically handicapped boy. In Armstrong's story, the boy looked out of a window toward an apple orchard and knew that he would never be able to run and play there. In fascination, he observed a pair of robins making their nest in one of the trees. Sometime later, he saw his pet cat climb into the tree and destroy the nest, killing the baby birds. When the parent birds returned to feed their young, they fluttered around in anguish, then flew away.

After reading Armstrong's story, the teacher requested that he stay after class. The other students left for the day, and the teacher asked him from where he had copied the story. Armstrong told the teacher that the story was his own work. The teacher did not believe him and took Armstrong and his story to the head of the English department and the headmaster of the school. Both school officials were sure that the story had been copied. However, Armstrong maintained that he had written the story. Years later, as a freshman in college, Armstrong submitted the same story to the literary magazine, and it was published.

Armstrong attended Augusta Military Academy and graduated with honors from Hampden-Sydney College. He married Martha Stonestreet Williams, who died in 1953. He is the father of three children: Christopher, David, and Mary. His home is in Kent, Connecticut. Armstrong was a history master at Kent School in Kent, and he used his love of history to write his stories.

Armstrong has written many stories and articles for magazines such as *Harper's* and *Barron's*. He wrote several books in addition to *Sounder*, such as *Barefoot In the Grass: The Story of Grandma Moses*, *Hadassah: the Orphan Queen*, and *Sour Land*. However, *Sounder* is without a doubt his most renowned work. It has been translated into eight languages and was made into a film, by Twentieth-Century Fox in 1972. *Sounder* won the Newbery Medal and the Lewis Carrol Shelf Award in 1970.

Sounder

by William H. Armstrong

Harper & Row, 1989

(Available in Canada and Australia from Harper Collins; in U.K. from Penguin.)

This story is about a poor "Negro" family. They lived in a small cabin which belonged to the white man who owned the land. The father of the family was a sharecropper for the white landowner. As winter approached, the family did not have enough food. The father went hunting for animals that could be eaten or whose pelts could be sold. He always took Sounder, his wonderful coon dog, when he went hunting. Sounder was a mixture of bulldog and hound. He was strong, tenacious, and an excellent hunter. When Sounder had an animal cornered or chased up a tree, he gave a distinctive, almost musical howl that could be heard throughout the hills of the countryside.

Even though the father and Sounder put forth their best effort, they frequently came home from hunting empty handed. In desperation, the father decided to steal a ham bone and some sausages. Just a few days after the theft three white men came to the sharecropper's cabin. They were the sheriff and two deputies. These men were extremely cruel and hateful as they arrested the father. The oldest son tried to hold onto Sounder, who became increasingly agitated by the way his master was being treated. However, Sounder escaped the boy's grasp and was shot by the sheriff. The father was taken away, and Sounder staggered off, possibly looking for a place to die.

The oldest boy was heartbroken by the loss of the two most important things in his life — his father, who always made him feel safe and unafraid, and Sounder, whom he adored and considered to be a member of the family. Every day the boy searched for Sounder. He also tried to find out where his father had been taken to serve a long sentence on a chain gang. He had no luck finding either one. Then one day Sounder appeared on the porch. Although his wounds had healed, they had left him deformed and partially crippled. A long time passed before the father was released from prison and allowed to return home. He had been injured in a dynamite explosion and was paralyzed on one side.

The oldest boy learned many hard lessons as he grew older. However, the kindness of a teacher he met while looking for his father changed his life forever.

Vocabulary Lists

On this page are vocabulary lists which correspond to each sectional grouping of chapters. Vocabulary activity ideas can be found on page 9 of this book.

SECTION 1
(Author's Note-Chapter I)

clapboard	eloquent
rafters	persimmon
calloused	burlap
chitlins	scythe
ajar	intoxication
addled	quarry
whetstone	treed
successive	sharecropper
heritage	coal oil
briar	ticking

SECTION 2
(Chapters II and III)

patchwork	spiraled
bramble	sowbelly
ashen	lunge
floundering	visualize
rivulets	evidence
fallow	pallet
mongrel	crockery
copperhead	threadbare
entangled	constrained
skittish	carcass

SECTION 3
(Chapters IV and V)

kernels	bulge
tannery	damper
corridor	stovepipe
famished	socket
quiver	chute
pressure	chain gang
poultice	perkish
chisel	vaccinate
mange	remote
Pharaoh	fret

SECTION 4
(Chapters VI and VII)

barbed wire	cistern
hobble	compulsion
gyration	gaunt
animosity	cowardice
sanctuary	conjured
remote	mellow
tote	malicious
baser	slosh
ornery	shaft
defiant	inhuman

SECTION 5
(Chapter VIII)

hobbled	sultry	parched	suffocate
sulfurous	insurance	mimic	crescent
resolve	weary	withered	deformed
amid	locust	drought	distinct
molest	Scriptures	rhythmic	avalanche

8

Vocabulary Activity Ideas

You can help your students learn and retain the vocabulary words in *Sounder* by providing them with interesting vocabulary activities. Here are a few ideas to try.

- Provide students with sentences, each containing a blank where a vocabulary word belongs. Have students **Use Context Clues** to fill in the blanks with the correct vocabulary words.

- Have students create an **Illustrated Class Dictionary** of the vocabulary words using a flip chart.

- On the chalkboard, list five vocabulary words to be **Words of the Day**. When students come into the classroom, have them use dictionaries to find the meanings of these words. Then have them share and discuss the meanings.

- Have students work in cooperative learning groups to **Write a Story** using as many of the vocabulary words as possible.

- Have students work with a partner to **Write Riddles** using the vocabulary words as the answers to the riddles. Ask students to share their riddles with the class.

- Challenge your students to a **Vocabulary Bee**. This is similar to a spelling bee, but in addition to spelling each word correctly, the game participants must correctly define the words as well.

- Ask students to create **Crossword Puzzles** or **Wordsearch Puzzles** using the vocabulary words from the story. Then puzzles can be duplicated so they can be shared with the entire class.

- Play **Twenty Clues** with the vocabulary words. In this game, a student gives clues about a vocabulary word, and the other students have twenty chances to guess what that word is. The student who correctly guesses the word gets to give the next set of clues.

- Have students make a **Part of Speech Categories Chart** with headings, such as Noun, Verb, Adjective, and Adverb. Under the appropriate heading, have them write each word in the context of a sentence, correctly showing its use as that part of speech.

- Play **Vocabulary Charades**. In this game, a student acts out the meaning of a vocabulary word while others try to guess what the word is.

- Divide the class into two teams. Ask both teams to **Locate a Vocabulary Word** in a section of the book. A team earns a point if they locate the word first. If that team can give the correct definition for the word, they earn another point. Continue playing with other vocabulary words. A team wins when they have the greatest number of points at the end of a period of time that you specify.

- You probably have many more ideas to add to this list. Try them! See if experiencing vocabulary on a personal level increases your students' vocabulary interest and retention.

Quiz Time!

1. On the back of this paper, write a one-paragraph summary of the major events in the Author's Note and the first chapter. Then complete the rest of the questions on this page.

2. How can you tell that this story takes place during a time when black people were not considered to be equal to white people?

   _____

   _____

3. What did the boy's father do for a living?

   _____

   _____

4. How would you describe Sounder?

   _____

   _____

5. Why was the dog named Sounder?

   _____

   _____

6. Why was Sounder important to the family?

   _____

   _____

7. What did the boy's mother do with the walnuts she cracked and shelled?

   _____

   _____

8. How did the boy feel when his father was at home?

   _____

   _____

9. What was unusual about the food the boy's mother cooked in the morning?

   _____

   _____

10. What did the boy want to have so that he would not be lonesome when his mother did not sing?

   _____

   _____

Shadow Puppetry

At the beginning of the story, the boy is on the porch with the two most important things in his life — his father, and Sounder, the coon dog. Although it is night, the dim light coming from the cabin creates shadows on the porch. In this activity, you will make a shadow puppet of Sounder to see what his shadow would look like on the porch.

Here are the materials you will need.

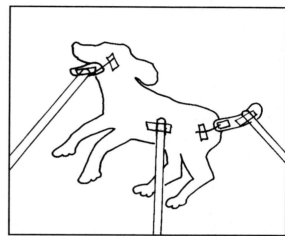

- a pencil
- a pair of scissors
- string or yarn
- a roll of tape
- a piece of tagboard
- three drinking straws
- white cloth or white paper (to be used as a screen)
- a lamp, with its shade removed

Here are the directions.

Step 1: Draw a fairly large picture of Sounder on the tagboard. Remember that Sounder is described as "a mixture of Georgia redbone hound and bulldog." He has a broad chest, strong neck muscles, and a square-shaped head and jaw.

Step 2: Cut out the picture you have drawn on the tagboard. Then cut off two parts that you want to be able to move on your puppet. You can choose to move the front and back legs or the tail and lower jaw.

Step 3: Connect the body to one of the parts you need to attach, such as the tail. Do this by taping one end of a small piece of string to the tail and the other end to the body where the tail belongs. Then do the same for the other part you need to attach.

Step 4: Tape the end of one straw to the middle of Sounder's body. Then tape the end of a straw to each of the moving parts. Now practice making your puppet move.

Step 5: Hang up the white cloth or white paper for the screen. Place the lamp near the screen.

Step 6: Turn on the lamp and turn off the other lights in the room. Place your puppet between the lamp and the screen. It should cast a shadow on the screen. Now make the shadow of your puppet move.

Anticipation Guide

Your students will better understand and enjoy a story if they prepare for reading a book by relating situations in the story to their personal experiences. This is particularly true of a book such as *Sounder*, because the story takes place during a period of American history with which students may not be familiar.

Before students begin reading *Sounder*, show them a copy of the book. Explain that they are going to read the book, but before they start they will give their opinions in response to some statements. Assure students that their answers will not be graded and that there are not any right or wrong answers.

After students have completed the anticipation guide, discuss their answers. Then collect the guides so they can be reviewed after students have finished reading the story. When students have completed the book, ask them to respond to the statements on the anticipation guide again. When they have completed the anticipation guide, return their original guide and have them compare the two. Ask students to describe how reading the book changed their opinions.

Anticipation Guide

Respond to the following statements with **agree** or **disagree.**

1. Every person has a right to food, shelter, and safety. _____

2. Only lazy people neglect to provide for their families. _____

3. The color of a person's skin can tell you a lot about what that person is like. _____

4. Stealing is always wrong, and a thief should always be punished severely. _____

5. A poor person who steals food should not be put in jail. _____

6. There is never a question about which choices are the right ones and which choices are the wrong ones. _____

7. Some people are born to lose. _____

8. Being able to attend school is a privilege. _____

From Slavery to Civil Rights

It is important to put a book like *Sounder* into historical perspective so that you can better understand the time period described in the story. Do research and take notes about the following events and people that have affected the lives of African Americans.

Slavery	**Brown v. Board of Education of Topeka**
Emancipation Proclamation	**Rosa Parks**
Sharecroppers	**De Facto Segregation**
Jim Crow Laws	**Martin Luther King, Jr.**
Plessy v. Ferguson	**Civil Rights Act of 1964**
De Jure Segregation	**Civil Rights Act of 1968**

Cut out the pages of the book shown below on the solid lines. Place the pages so that one is on top of the other. Fold them on the dotted line and staple to form a miniature book that will be about African American history. Leave the front page blank so that you can make a cover when you are finished. Write the name of an event or person at the top of each page. Complete each page by telling about the event or person, using the information that you gathered doing your research. The first one is done for you.

<table>
<tr>
<td></td>
<td>Leave blank for cover</td>
</tr>
<tr>
<td></td>
<td>

Slavery

European traders regularly went to Africa during the 1500s through the 1800s. The traders captured millions of African men, women, and children. The Africans were sent by ship to the colonies in the New World, where they were sold as slaves. The slaves usually had to work on plantations, which were large farms, or in mines.

</td>
</tr>
<tr>
<td></td>
<td></td>
</tr>
</table>

Reading Response Journals

One effective way to insure that the reading of *Sounder* touches each student in a personal way is to include the use of Reading Response Journals in your plans. In these journals, students can be encouraged to respond to the story in a number of ways. Here are a few ideas.

- Ask students to create a journal for *Sounder*. Tell them that the purpose of the journal is to record their thoughts, ideas, observations, and questions as they read *Sounder*.

- Provide students with, or ask them to suggest, topics from the story that would stimulate writing. Here are a few examples from the chapter in Section 1.

  — Describe what life was like for the son of a sharecropper. Do you think that the boy's life would have been different if he were the son of the white landowner? Explain your answer.

  — Describe how the boy felt about Sounder. What clues in the story led you to this conclusion?

  — How did the boy's mother get the sausages and the ham bone that she was cooking?

  — Why do you think learning to read was so important to the boy? Why is being able to read important to you?

- Before beginning a section of the story, provide a question for students to think about while they read. The questions should require students to use higher-level thinking skills while helping them focus on a particular aspect of the text.

- After reading each chapter, students can write one or more new things they learned. Ask students to draw their responses to certain events or characters in the story, using the blank pages in their journals.

- Tell students that they may use their journals to record "diary-type" responses that they want to enter. Encourage students to bring their journal ideas to life! Ideas generated from their journal writing can be used to create plays, debates, stories, songs, and art displays.

- Allow students time to share things that they have written or drawn in their journals. This can be done as a class or in small groups. Before beginning, be sure to ask students not to be critical of each other's work.

Allow students time to write in their journals daily. Non-judgmental teacher responses should be made as you read the journals to let the students know you are reading and enjoying what they have written. Here are some types of responses that will encourage your students to write more.

  — "You have really found what's important in the story!"

  — "You have made some very interesting comments. Do you mind if I share your ideas with the class?"

Quiz Time!

1. On the back of this paper, write a one-paragraph summary of the major events in each chapter of this section. Then complete the rest of the questions on this page.

2. How long did the boy's house smell like ham bone?

_____

_____

3. Who were the visitors who came to the boy's house, and why did they come?

_____

_____

4. What did the white man mean when he called the boy's father "boy"?

_____

_____

5. How did Sounder get shot?

_____

_____

6. Why did the boy's mother call him back from following Sounder?

_____

_____

7. What did the boy mean when he called Sounder a "human animal"?

_____

_____

8. Where did the boy's mother go the next morning, and what did she take with her?

_____

_____

9. What did the boy find in the road where Sounder had been shot? What did the boy do with it, and what happened to it?

_____

_____

10. How did the house feel to the boy when he was left in charge of the younger children?

_____

_____

A Crossword Puzzle

Create a crossword puzzle, using information from the story as the clues. The answers to the clues should be single words. The first one has been done for you. Color in any boxes of the puzzle that you do not need. Then have a friend solve your puzzle.

¹S	O	U	N	D	E	R							

ACROSS

1. The name of the boy's dog

_____

_____

_____

_____

_____

_____

DOWN

_____

_____

_____

_____

_____

_____

Be a Detective

In *Sounder*, the father was arrested for stealing a ham bone and some sausages. The only real piece of evidence found at the scene of the crime was "threads of torn cloth." As a result of this one small clue, the sheriff and deputies felt free to push their way into the cabin and arrest the father.

Today detectives carefully establish the guilt of a criminal using a variety of clues. They know how to find many kinds of evidence at a crime scene. Among other things, detectives look for fingerprints. Each person's fingerprints are unique. This means that no two people have exactly the same fingerprints.

In this activity, you will pretend that you are at a school that trains detectives. You will try to match fingerprints with the five or six students who made them.

Here are the materials you will need.

- sheets of blank paper
- index cards
- a copy of the chart shown below
- one or two ink pads

Here are the directions for the activity.

Step 1: Pick one student to be the instructor for the detectives. All of the others will be the student detectives.

Step 2: Have the instructor turn away from the student detectives or temporarily leave the room.

Step 3: Have the student detectives use the stamp pad and some sheets of blank paper to practice making fingerprints of their right index fingers without smearing them.

In the mean time, have the instructor look at the sample chart shown below and use a sheet of paper to make a "Police Records" chart that has a space for the name and fingerprint of each student detective.

Name of Student Detective	Right Index Finger

Step 4: Have the student detectives take an index card. On one side of the card, they should write their names. On the other side, they should carefully make fingerprints of their right index fingers. (If a fingerprint smears, redo it on a clean card.)

Step 5: Place all of the cards on a table so that only the side with the fingerprints can be seen.

Step 6: Ask the instructor to turn around or return to the room. Have the instructor ask the student detectives to write their names and place their fingerprints on the "Police Records" chart.

Step 7: The instructor compares the fingerprints on the index cards with those on the chart and tries to determine which fingerprint belongs to which student detective. The captain checks the answers by turning over the index cards.

Step 8: Redo the activity as many times as you like, allowing different students to be the instructor.

Riddles

The boy's mother goes to the store to sell the walnut kernels. She leaves the oldest boy in charge of the younger children. Before the boy goes out to look for Sounder, he asks the children this riddle. 'If you're inside you look out, and if you're outside you look in, but what looks both ways?' Since none of the children says anything he tells them, 'The window is the answer; it looks both ways.'

Create eight riddles of your own. Write one riddle in each box shown below. Then cut the boxes out to make riddle cards. On the backs of the cards write the answers to the riddles. Then give the cards to some friends and see if they can solve your riddles.

?	?
?	?
?	?
?	?

Before and After

There are certain events which happen in everyone's life that change that person forever. In this section of the story, such an event happened to the boy. In the circle labeled "Before," write a list of words and phrases that describe the boy's life before the white men came to the cabin. In the circle labeled "After," write words and phrases that describe the boy's life after the white men left the cabin.

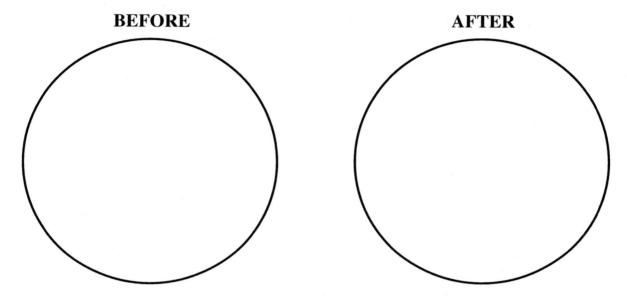

BEFORE   **AFTER**

Now, think of an event that has changed your life. In the circle labeled "Before," write a list of words and phrases that describe your life before the event, and in the circle labeled "After," write a list of words and phrases that describe your life since the event.

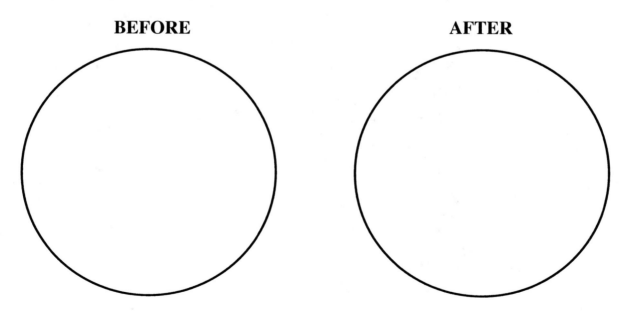

BEFORE   **AFTER**

Quiz Time!

1. On the back of this paper, write a one-paragraph summary of the major events in each chapter of this section. Then complete the rest of the questions on this page.

2. Why did the boy tell the younger children not to ask their mother for stick candy?

   _____

   _____

3. Where did the boy's mother think Sounder had gone and why?

   _____

   _____

4. What did the boy's mother bring from the store?

   _____

5. Why did the boy's mother tell him that he must learn to lose?

   _____

   _____

   _____

6. Why did the man with the red face break the cake?

   _____

7. How did the boy feel on his way to town, and how did he feel on his way home?

   _____

   _____

   _____

8. Why do you think the boy's father told him not to come again?

   _____

   _____

9. What did Sounder look like when the boy found him on the porch the morning after seeing his father in jail?

   _____

   _____

10. What punishment did the court order for the boy's father?

   _____

   _____

Bake a Cake

The mother put a great deal of love into making the cake she sent to her husband for Christmas. A cake was something special because many of its ingredients were so expensive. The mother had to laboriously crack and shell walnuts for many nights in order to get enough money to buy the ingredients for the cake. In this activity, you will make a cake like the one the mother made. Be sure to work with adult supervision and follow all kitchen safety rules.

Here are the ingredients for the vanilla buttercream icing.

- 1 cup (236 mL) confectioners' sugar
- 1¹/₂ (23 mL) tablespoons butter
- 1 teaspoon (5 mL) vanilla

Here are the ingredients for the cake.

- 1 cup (236 mL) granulated sugar
- ¹/₄ cup (59 mL) butter (softened)
- 2 eggs
- 1 teaspoon (5 mL) vanilla
- 1²/₃ cups (393 mL) sifted cake flour
- 2¹/₂ teaspoons (13 mL) baking powder
- ¹/₂ teaspoon (3 mL) salt
- ¹/₂ cup (118 mL) whole milk
- fruit jam (optional)

Here are the directions for making the icing.

Step 1: Make the icing before you make the cake so that it will be easier to spread and will not have a raw taste.

Step 2: In a mixing bowl, beat the butter until it is soft.

Step 3: Gradually sift the sugar into the bowl with the butter. Blend the mixture until it is creamy.

Step 4: Stir in the vanilla. If the icing is too thin, sift in a little more sugar until it is thicker.

Step 5: Place the bowl over a pot of hot water. Allow it to set until the cake is completely cooled.

Here are the directions for making the cake.

Step 1: Sift the sugar into a large mixing bowl. Gradually add the softened butter to the sugar. Blend until creamy.

Step 2: Beat the eggs in, one at a time, and add the vanilla.

Step 3: In a separate bowl, sift the cake flour with the baking powder and the salt. Alternate between adding ¹/₃ of the flour mixture and then ¹/₃ of the milk until they have both been completely added to the butter mixture.

Step 4: Use butter or vegetable oil to grease two round 9-inch (23 cm) cake pans. Pour an equal amount of batter into each pan.

Step 5: Bake at 375 degrees Fahrenheit (190°Celsius) for about 25 minutes.

Step 6: Allow the layers to completely cool and then remove them from the pans.

Step 7: Spread fruit jam or vanilla buttercream icing between layers. Cover the sides and top of the cake with vanilla buttercream icing.

A Mock Trial

In this activity, you are going to pretend that the father in *Sounder* has been accused of stealing in modern times. Today, he is guaranteed the right to a fair trial. Work together with a group of students to present a mock trial. In a mock trial, just as in a real trial, a person's participation in a crime is debated. Students in your group will need to take the following parts in the mock trial.

Prosecutor: The prosecutor is the attorney who speaks for the victims or the local, state, or federal government. This attorney attempts to convince the jury that the person accused of a crime is guilty.

Defense Attorney: The defense attorney tries to convince the jury that the person accused of a crime is not guilty. If the accused cannot afford to pay attorney fees, an attorney, called a public defender, is appointed and the fees are paid by the taxpayers.

Defendant: The defendant is the person accused of a crime. The defendant is always presumed innocent until proven guilty. The burden of presenting this proof is on the prosecutor.

Victim: The victim is the person whom the crime was committed against.

Judge: The judge is the person in charge of the trial. The judge is responsible for making sure the court's proceedings are legal and explaining any questions about the law to the jury.

Jury: The jury consists of twelve people (jurors) who are selected to hear all the evidence and decide whether the defendant is guilty or not guilty. The jurors must remain impartial throughout the trial and make a decision based only on the facts presented. They are instructed by the judge to give a verdict of "not guilty" if there is "reasonable doubt" about whether the defendant committed the crime.

Witnesses for the Defense: These witnesses are the people who testify on behalf of the defendant.

Witnesses for the Prosecution: These witnesses are the people who testify against the defendant.

Take time to plan your mock trial carefully. Remember the purpose of a trial is to determine if the defendant is guilty or not guilty of a crime. You do not have to establish the defendant's innocence. After the mock trial, use the back of this paper to describe what you learned from it.

The Bill of Rights

The Bill of Rights consists of the first ten Amendments to the Constitution. These Amendments describe the rights of all American citizens. Use a reference book to locate a copy of the Bill of Rights. Read each Amendment, explain the meaning in your own words, then tell why you think it is important.

First Amendment
What does it mean? _____
Why is it important?_____

Second Amendment
What does it mean? _____
Why is it important?_____

Third Amendment
What does it mean? _____
Why is it important?_____

Fourth Amendment
What does it mean? _____
Why is it important?_____

Fifth Amendment
What does it mean? _____
Why is it important?_____

Sixth Amendment
What does it mean? _____
Why is it important?_____

Seventh Amendment
What does it mean? _____
Why is it important?_____

Eighth Amendment
What does it mean? _____
Why is it important?_____

Ninth Amendment
What does it mean? _____
Why is it important?_____

Tenth Amendment
What does it mean? _____
Why is it important?_____

Write Your Own Song

The boy's mother often sings the words, "You gotta walk that lonesome valley." The boy recognizes this old spiritual as her song because she has sung it so often. He knows that singing this song helps his mother cope with the sorrow and anxiety in her life.

Many people, like the boy's mother, enjoy singing songs that were written long ago while others prefer to write their own songs. One kind of song that you can write is called a ballad. A ballad tells a story and has a rhyming pattern and a definite rhythm, or beat. An example of this type of song is "The Ballad of John Henry." This ballad is very old. Consequently, several different versions of it have been created over the years. The first verse of one version is shown below.

*When John **Henry was** a little-bitty **boy,***
*No **big**ger than the **palm** of your **han',***
*He **picked** up a **ham**mer and a **little piece** of **steel,***
*Said John **Hen**ry gonna be a **steel-dri**ving **man,***
Lord, Lord!
*John **Hen**ry gonna be a **steel-dri**ving **man!***

This verse tells the beginning of John Henry's story. He was a man who worked for the railroad by hammering in the steel spikes that held down the train tracks. When John Henry was alive, this back-breaking job was done by human labor before a machine was invented that could do it. He believed he could drive the spikes into the tracks faster than a newly invented machine. According to the story, John Henry died trying to prove this.

If you read the first verse of the ballad without stressing any words or syllables, you might have gotten a sense of its rhythm from the rhyming of han' and man. However, you may not have realized the rhythm was intended to sound like a man striking heavy blows with a sledge hammer, keeping time almost like a machine. Reread the ballad. This time try to stress the words and syllables that are **boldfaced.**

In this activity, you will write your own ballad.

1. Think of a simple story to tell. Novels, newspapers, or magazines can be excellent sources for story ideas.
2. Write four lines for each verse. You may wish to create your own rhyme scheme or use one of these: rhyme lines 1 and 2, then 3 and 4; rhyme lines 1 and 3, then 2 and 4; rhyme lines 1 and 4, then 2 and 3.
3. Repeat any line that you wish to stress and you think helps create the rhythm of the ballad.
4. Practice singing your ballad in front of a mirror before you perform it for the class.

Quiz Time!

1. On the back of this paper, write a one-paragraph summary of the major events in each chapter of this section. Then complete the rest of the questions on this page.

2. How did the boy spend his days in the spring?

_____

_____

3. Why did the boy take journeys so far from home?

_____

_____

4. What did the boy find thrown into the trash barrels of the towns he went through? Why did he think these were wonderful?

_____

_____

5. Why did the boy listen to the wind?

_____

_____

6. How long has the boy's father been on the chain gang?

_____

_____

7. What happened to the boy's hand?

_____

_____

8. How did the boy know his father was not on the chain gang whitewashing rocks?

_____

_____

9. What did the boy do with the book that he found in the trash?

_____

_____

10. What kinds of things amazed the boy when he was in the old teacher's house?

_____

_____

Diorama of a Schoolhouse

The boy stopped at a schoolhouse to wash the blood off his hand where the guard had injured it. It is there that he met the old, white-haired teacher. In this activity, you will make a diorama of the schoolhouse. A diorama shows a setting in miniature. Reread the description of the schoolhouse in Chapter VII so you will know what your diorama should look like. You may also wish to include the boy, other children, the teacher, the dogs, and the pig.

Here is what you will need to make a diorama of the schoolhouse.

- a rectangular box (preferably a shoebox) with a lid
- a pair of scissors
- cardboard, construction paper, fabric, cellophane, wood, clay, aluminum foil, etc.
- glue

Here are the directions for how to make your diorama of the schoolhouse.

Step 1: Use your scissors to cut a peephole that is about $1/2$ inch (1.27 cm) in diameter in the center of one short side of the box.

Step 2: Create your background scenery and glue it onto the end of the box that is opposite the peephole.

Step 3: Use a variety of materials to create the school, characters, and objects for your diorama. You may want to draw a sketch for yourself so you will know where to place these in your diorama.

Step 4: Glue the school, characters, and objects to the bottom and sides of the box. As you are gluing, be sure to look in the peephole occasionally to see how your diorama looks. Allow the glue to dry.

Step 5: Create a sky by decorating the inside of the box lid. Allow the glue to dry. Then place the lid on the box. If you need additional light in your diorama, try cutting some slits in the top of the box. You can create some special effects with the lighting by covering the slits with wax paper or tissue paper.

Peep Hole

Present a Skit

A very effective way to experience what you read is to present a skit of a scene from the book. Work with three or four other students to pick a scene that you would like to present as a skit. Use the following organizer to help plan your skit.

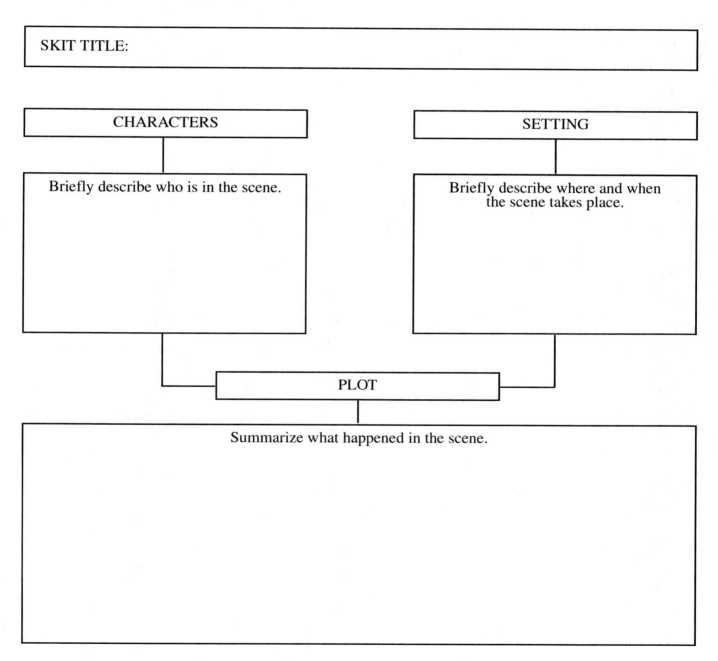

SKIT TITLE:

CHARACTERS

Briefly describe who is in the scene.

SETTING

Briefly describe where and when the scene takes place.

PLOT

Summarize what happened in the scene.

As you work together to write your skit, you may want to include the use of a few special props or some simple scenery. After the skit is written, rehearse it several times. Practice speaking loudly and clearly so the audience will be able to understand you. When everyone in your group feels comfortable performing their parts, present your skit to the class.

A Newspaper Article

In this section, some people read a newspaper article to the boy's mother about a terrible accident that happened at one of the quarries. There was a dynamite blast in which 12 convicts had been killed and several others wounded. The boy's father was not named as one of the dead convicts.

Pretend you are the newspaper reporter who was asked to write the article about the accident at the quarry. Use the space below to write your article. Write a headline, or title, that will make people want to read it. In your article, be sure you answer these questions: who, what, when, where, how, and why. To make your article seem more realistic, you may wish to include quotes from the quarry guards who witnessed the explosion.

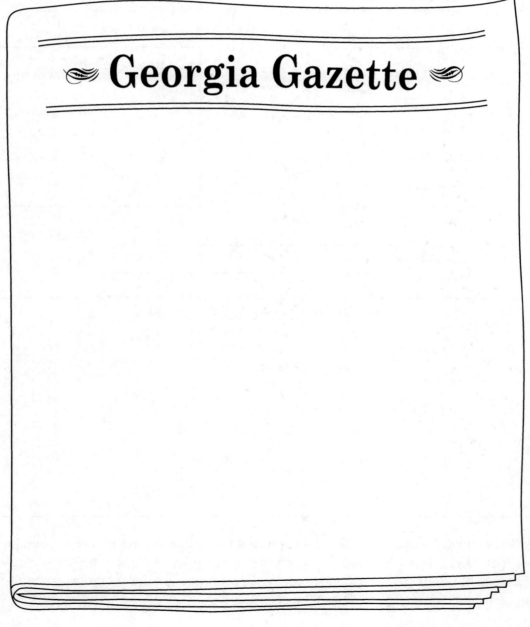

Georgia Gazette

Coping Strategies

Sometimes things happen in life that make us feel frightened, worried, or upset. In order to respond to situations like these, we develop coping strategies. Knowing how to cope helps us survive these stressful times.

The characters in *Sounder* must find ways to cope with stressful situations, too. For example, the boy can always tell when his mother is worried about something because she hums. Fill in the boxes below to provide an example from this section of the story that shows how a character deals with a stressful situation.

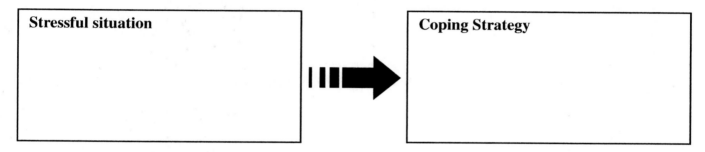

Stressful situation

Coping Strategy

Now, think of three different times that you had to cope with a stressful situation in your life. Use the boxes below to describe the situations and the coping strategies you used.

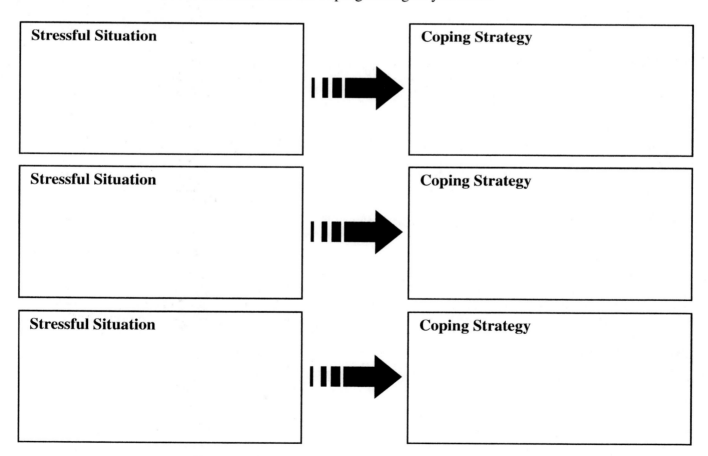

Stressful Situation

Coping Strategy

Stressful Situation

Coping Strategy

Stressful Situation

Coping Strategy

Quiz Time!

1. On the back of this paper, write a one-paragraph summary of the major events in this chapter. Then complete the rest of the questions on this page.

2. Who did the boy tell his mother and the children about when he came home from searching for his father? Why did he tell them about this person?

_____

_____

3. Why did the mother let the boy go to live with someone she had never met?

_____

_____

4. After starting school, how did the boy divide up his time each year?

_____

_____

5. How many years passed between the time the father was carried away and when he returned? How can you tell?

_____

_____

6. Why did the mother think the "dog days" of summer are bad?

_____

_____

7. What did Sounder suddenly do when he recognized the person who was walking down the road?

_____

_____

8. Who was the person walking down the road toward the cabin?

_____

9. What happened to the boy's father while he worked at the prison quarry?

_____

_____

10. What do you think the teacher meant when he said that "if a flower blooms once, it goes on blooming somewhere forever"?

_____

_____

Make a Board Game

Work with three or four other students to make a board game using information from *Sounder*. First, prepare a set of 3-inch by 5-inch (8 cm by 13 cm) game cards with questions from the story. Include the answers on the cards. Second, glue the game board shown below onto a piece of posterboard. After the glue dries, decorate the game board using ideas from the story. Third, obtain a die or a number cube and game tokens. Fourth, write down a set of rules for the game. Be sure the game cards are read aloud by someone other than the player whose turn it is.

Prejudice

People who are prejudiced dislike a person or group of people without a good reason. In *Sounder*, many of the white people were prejudiced against African Americans. These white people did not believe that African Americans deserved to have equal rights. As a result, African Americans were often humiliated and treated cruelly.

Work with three or four other students to discuss prejudice. Have group members select one of these jobs: one person reads the questions listed below, one person records the group's ideas, one person gathers the materials needed to make the poster, and one or two others report to the class. Be sure that everyone in your group gets to participate, and remember to be polite when listening to others share their ideas.

Here are some questions you should discuss with your group. Record your group's ideas on a separate sheet of paper.

1. Before the Civil War, how do you think slavery affected white people's attitudes toward African Americans?

2. Before the Civil War, how do you think slavery affected the self-concept of African Americans?

3. After the Civil War, why do you think some white people were prejudiced against African Americans?

4. After the Civil War, do you think any of the African Americans were prejudiced against white people? Explain your answer.

5. Do you think there are any people today who are prejudiced against African Americans? Explain your answer.

6. Do you think there are any African Americans today who are prejudiced against other groups of people? Explain your answer.

7. Do you think there are any people today who are prejudiced against groups other than African Americans? Explain your answer.

8. What do you think causes people to be prejudiced?

9. Has anyone ever been prejudiced against you? If so, tell about your experience.

10. What could you do if you knew someone was prejudiced?

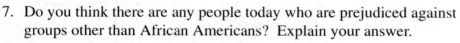

After completing the questions, work together to design a poster that shows some peaceful ways to overcome prejudice. Use the back of this paper to plan your poster. It can include pictures and words. When you are ready to make your poster, obtain crayons or markers and a piece of poster board. After completing your poster, share it and your group's responses to the questions with the class.

Georgia

Sounder takes place in Georgia. To learn more about this state, look for maps of Georgia in atlases, road atlases, encyclopedias, or other reference books. Then, follow the directions shown below to locate and label some places and geographic features on this map of Georgia.

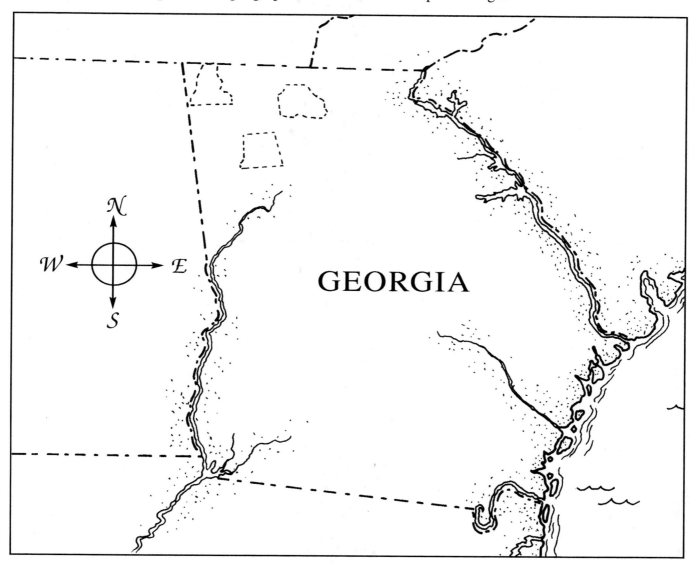

1. Locate and label the five states that border Georgia.
2. Locate, color, and label Gilmer County, Bartow County, and Walker County.
3. Locate the river that forms part of the western boundary of Georgia. Color it blue and label it.
4. Locate the river that forms part of the eastern boundary of Georgia. Color it blue and label it.
5. Locate the river that forms part of the southern boundary of Georgia. Color it blue and label it.
6. Locate the ocean that lies to the east of Georgia. Color it blue and label it.
7. Locate the capital of Georgia. Draw a star where it belongs and label it.
8. Locate and label a mountain range that is in the northwest corner of Georgia.

Dear Mr. Armstrong

Authors like to hear from the people who read their books. Write a letter to William H. Armstrong telling him what you liked or disliked about *Sounder*. Tell him how you felt while you were reading the book. Try to express your appreciation for his craft as a writer.

When writing your letter, be sure to include the parts labeled in the following diagram of a letter.

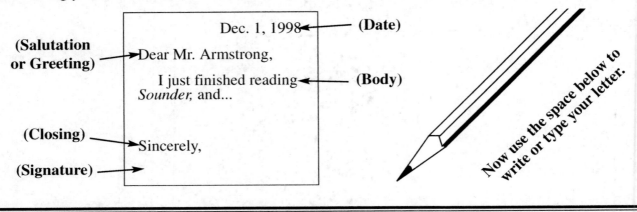

Any Questions?

When you finished reading *Sounder*, did you have any questions that were left unanswered? Write some of your questions here.

_____

_____

_____

_____

_____

_____

Work in groups, or by yourself, to prepare possible answers for the questions you have asked above and those written below. When you have finished your responses, share your ideas with the class.

- Why was learning how to read so important to the boy?

- How long did the boy live with the white-haired old man who was his teacher?

- How did the boy get to be a teacher?

- Later in life, did the boy ever return to visit the gravesites of Sounder and his father?

- Did the boy live long enough to see African Americans have equal rights?

- Did the boy ever marry and have a family of his own?

- How did the boy deal with the anger he felt toward people who mistreated him and his father?

- What happened to the younger children in the sharecropper's family?

- Did the younger children have the opportunity to go to school?

- Did the boy teach them how to read and write?

- Did any of the sharecropper's children break the law and have to go to prison?

- What did the mother do after all of the children grew up and left home?

- Did the mother live long enough to see African Americans have equal rights?

- Were the sheriff or deputies ever punished for their treatment of African American prisoners?

- Were the prison guards ever punished for their cruel treatment of prisoners?

- When did the use of chain gangs come to an end? If so, why were they discontinued?

- Did the white people in the boy's town ever change their attitudes toward African Americans?

- Were there any white people who spoke out against the unfair treatment of African Americans?

Book Report Ideas

There are numerous ways to create a book report. After you have finished reading *Sounder*, choose one method of reporting that interests you. It may be a way that your teacher suggests, an idea of your own, or one of the ways mentioned below.

- **The Updated Version**

  Make a chart that shows how the story events might change if they took place in modern times as opposed to the post-Civil War time period.

- **Write an Autobiography**

  Imagine that you are the boy. Write an autobiography of your life, beginning with your family before your father was taken away and extending until you become a teacher.

- **Literary Interview**

  With a friend, conduct an interview of one of the characters in *Sounder*. One of you will take the part of the character. The other will take the part of the interviewer, providing the audience with insights into the character's personality and life. You are both responsible for creating meaningful questions and appropriate responses.

- **See What I Read?**

  This report is a visual one. A model of a scene from the story can be created, or a likeness of one or more of the characters from the story can be drawn or sculpted.

- **Guess Who or What!**

  This report is similar to the game "Twenty Questions." The reporter gives a series of general to specific clues about an event or character from the story. Other students guess which event or character is being described.

- **A Character Comes to Life!**

  Suppose one of the characters in *Sounder* came to life and walked into your home or classroom. This report describes what this characters sees, hears, and feels as he or she experiences the world in which you live.

- **A Letter to a Character**

  In this report, you may write a letter to any character in the story. You may want to ask that character questions or offer some advice on a particular problem that arises in the story.

- **Role-Playing**

  This report is one that lends itself to a group project. Work with three or four other students to role-play a scene from the story. You may wish to use costumes and props that will help the scene come to life. After performing the scene, explain why it is an important part of the story.

- **Become a Character in the Story**

  Rewrite your favorite part of the story, adding yourself as one of the characters.

Research Ideas

Describe three things that you read in *Sounder* that you would like to learn more about.

1. _____

2. _____

3. _____

As you read *Sounder*, you encountered different types of people, geographical locations, and prejudice. To increase your understanding of the time period, characters, and events in *Sounder* and to help you better appreciate William H. Armstrong's craft as a writer, research to learn more about these people, places, events, and things.

Work in groups to research one or more of the areas you named above, or the areas that are mentioned below. Share your findings with the rest of the class in any appropriate form of oral presentation.

Animals
- Georgia redbone hound
- Bulldog
- Raccoons
- Possums
- Snakes
  - Dry-land moccasin
  - Copperhead
- Foxes
- Squirrels
- Weasels
- Birds
  - Catbirds
  - Mockingbirds

History
- Slavery
- Sharecropping
- Segregation
- Education
- Prison labor
  - Road camps
  - Quarries
  - State farms
  - Chain gangs
- Georgia

Plants
- Persimmon tree
- Wild grapevine
- Cottonwoods
- Jack oaks
- Walnuts
- Mistletoe
- Bittersweet berries
- Lilac
- Locust

Bible Stories
- Noah's ark
- King David
- Joseph
- Moses
- Abraham
- Jacob

Other
- Natural phenomena
- Shadows
- Clouds
- Sea foam
- Drought
- Heat waves

Make a Big Book

Sounder is a story that can be enjoyed by people of all ages. In this activity, you will make a Big Book of *Sounder* and use it to tell the story to younger students. Work with two or three other students in your class to pick one important event from each chapter that you could show in a picture. Use the boxes below to plan the eight pictures you will draw for your big book. You can plan the pictures using sketches or write phrases that describe what they will look like.

After you have planned your pictures, obtain five pieces of white posterboard. If only one side of the posterboard is white, glue white butcher paper to the back so that both sides are white. Use one side of a piece of posterboard to create a cover for your book. Be sure to include the title, author, and your group members' names. On the back of your cover, draw or paint the picture of the first event you want to show. On the front and back of a second piece of posterboard, draw or paint the second and third events you want to show. Continue until you have completed drawing or painting your eight events. The back of the posterboard with the eighth event will be blank and act like a back cover. Place the pieces of posterboard in order according to the story events. Punch holes and bind the big book with yarn or metal rings.

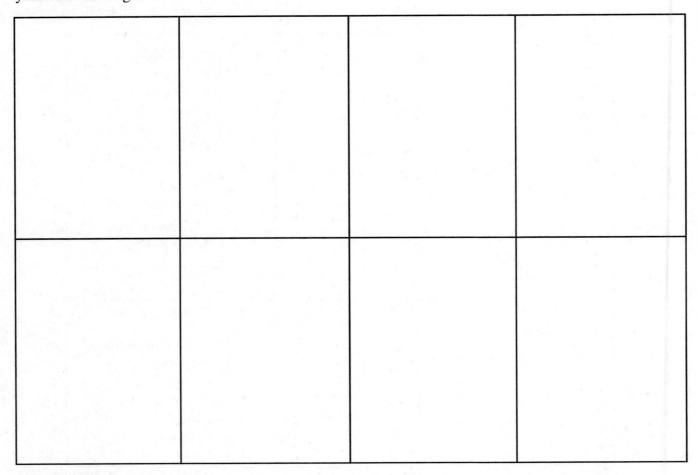

Now that your group has finished making the Big Book, you are ready to tell the story. For an explanation of how to become storytellers, read page 39.

Become Storytellers

Here are some ideas to help your group prepare to become storytellers. When you are ready, use your big book to tell the story of *Sounder* to some younger students.

Make an Outline: Plan an outline of your script around the pictures in your big book. Group members should decide who will provide the voices for the narrator and each of the different characters. Be sure to include dialogue between the characters. You will use your own words to tell the story, so it will change a little bit each time you tell it. You do not need to memorize specific lines; just know the main ideas that go into making the story.

Be Dramatic: As group members speak for the characters, they should change the tone of their voice to reflect different emotions. You can create suspense by pausing at appropriate times as you tell the story.

Use Props and Costumes: You may wish to use some simple props and costumes to make the story seem more real. Examples — An empty box can be shown as the box in which the mother put the cake for the father. The group member providing the voice for the mother could wear an apron.

Provide Sound Effects: Sound effects can be created during the telling of the story, or they can be recorded on a cassette tape. For example, you could record the slamming of a door to use when telling about what happened to the boy when he left the jail in which his father was being held.

Arrange the Seating: Place the chairs that you will sit in as you tell the story so that each group member can be easily seen and there is plenty of room to turn the pages in the big book.

Consider Using Music: You may wish to include background music, or have the group member who provides the voice for the mother hum or sing at appropriate times during the telling of the story.

Think about the Audience: When telling the story, be sure to speak clearly and loudly so that everyone in the audience can understand what is being said. Try not to tell the story too quickly, or young students will have difficulty following the plot. Do not make the story too long, or they will lose interest.

Plan to Rehearse: Telling the story as a group practice several times. Practicing in front of a mirror sometimes helps build confidence.

Make Arrangements: After all of the group members feel comfortable telling the story, schedule a time to tell it to a class of younger students.

Character Traits

When reading *Sounder*, our mental image of the characters is incredibly vivid, even though the author has created all but the dog without giving them names. Work with three or four other students to brainstorm a list of words and phrases that describe each of the following characters: the mother, the father, the boy, Sounder, the guard at the jail, the old white-haired teacher. Write the descriptive words in the appropriate oval shown below.

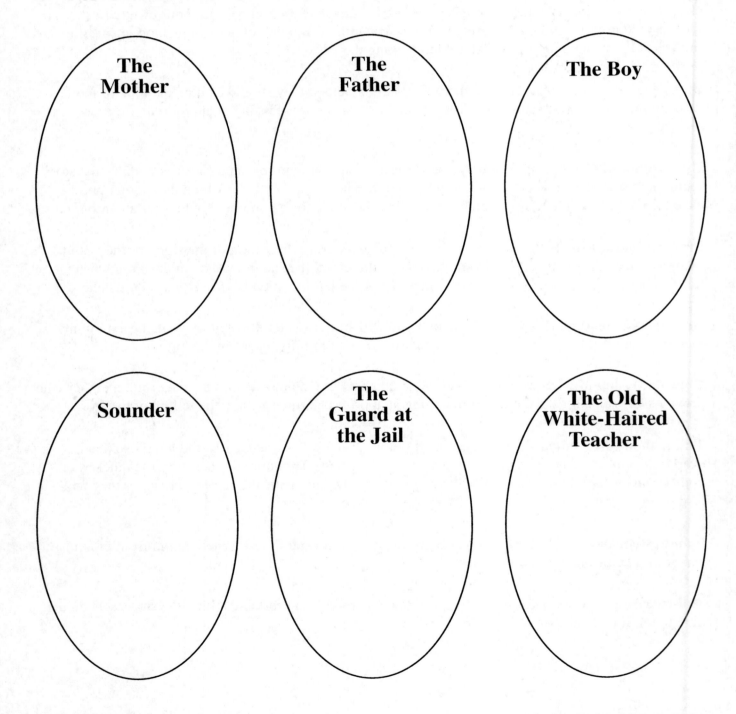

Sounder on Video

You can enhance the study of a novel such as *Sounder* by having students watch the video version of the story. Use some of the following group activities in conjunction with the presentation of the video.

- Stop the video and have students predict what will happen next.

- Stop the video and ask students to brainstorm some alternate outcomes for story events.

- Have students make a Venn diagram to compare and contrast the video to the book.

- Have students make a chart that shows what information was in the book but not the video and what information was in the video but not the book.

- Have students pretend to be movie critics. Have them describe what they liked and disliked about the video. Be sure they give specific examples.

- Have students take notes about the sequence of events shown on the video. Ask them to use their notes to make a timeline of story events.

- Take a poll to find out how many students enjoyed the book more than the video and how many enjoyed the video more than the book. Have students graph the results of the poll.

- Have students view the video sequel to *Sounder* which is called *Part 2, Sounder*. Ask them to debate which video was better. Be sure they give specific reasons why they believe one is better than the other.

- Have students consider how the presentation of the story would have to be changed if it were a play with live actors performing *Sounder*.

- After reading the book and viewing the video, have students work in cooperative learning groups to role-play important events in the story. Use a video camera to record each group's presentation to the class. Have students compare and contrast their video with the professional version.

- Play the video without sound. Have students take turns narrating the story as the video plays.

Unit Test

Matching: Match these quotes with the characters who said them.

the teacher	the mother	the deputy
the guard	the father	the boy

1. _____ *'Sounder and me must be about the same age,...'*

2. _____ *'Get that dog out of the way and hold him if you don't want him dead.'*

3. _____ *'Some people is born to keep. Some is born to lose.'*

4. _____ *'Tell her I'll send word with the visitin' preacher.'*

5. _____ *'Wait 'til I get my papers and lock the door, and I'll take you home and fix it.'*

True or False: Write true or false next to each statement below.

1. _____ Sounder was injured in a hunting accident.

2. _____ The father was arrested for stealing a ham bone and pork sausages.

3. _____ The mother could not visit the father while he was in prison because women were not allowed in the jail.

4. _____ The boy went to visit his father many times while he was in prison.

5. _____ The father was injured in a dynamite explosion.

Short Answer: Provide a short answer for each of these questions.

1. What kind of work did the father do? _____

2. Why did the mother think Sounder had gone to the woods after being shot? _____

_____

3. Why did the guard at the jail destroy the cake the mother had baked for the father? _____

_____

4. How does the boy get the opportunity to go to school? _____

_____

5. Why did Sounder not bark while the father was away in prison? _____

_____

Essay: Answer these essay questions on the back of this paper.

1. What are three examples of prejudice from the story? Why do you think some white people had such strong feelings of prejudice against African Americans?

2. How are Sounder and the father alike? How are they different?

Response

Explain the meanings of these quotations from *Sounder*.

Chapter I: *It wavered through the foothills, louder than any dog's in the whole countryside.*

Chapter I: *...the boy's mother was cutting wedge-shaped pieces of corn mush from an iron pot that stood on the back of the stove.*

Chapter I: *He did not take the lantern or Sounder or the boy with him.*

Chapter II: *'If you want to swing on a gate, boy, swing on the one behind the house.'*

Chapter II: *Sounder lay still in the road.*

Chapter II: *The loneliness that was always in the cabin, except when his mother was singing or telling a story about the Lord, was heavier than ever now.*

Chapter III: *In the morning the boy's mother did not cook any pork sausage for breakfast.*

Chapter IV: *'She won't bring no stick candy. Don't ask her for none.'*

Chapter IV: *'But you must learn to lose, child.'*

Chapter IV: *'This could have a steel file or hacksaw blade in it,...'*

Chapter IV: *Then the horse doctor had gotten mad and said, 'Get a chain. I'll make him stand still.'*

Chapter V: *Would his father send word with the visiting preacher where he had gone?*

Chapter V: *He dreamed that a wonderful man had come up to him as he was trying to read the store signs aloud and had said, 'Child, you want to learn, don't you?'*

Chapter V: *'Poor creature. Poor creature,' said the mother and turned away to get him some food.*

Chapter VI: *'To the end of the county might be a far journey, and out of the county would be a far, far journey, but I'll go,' the boy thought.*

Chapter VI: *'What you doing, kid, seeing how you gonna like it when you grow up?'*

Chapter VI: *When David moved his army around into the hills to attack his enemy, he heard the mighty roar of the wind moving in the tops of the trees, and he cried out to his men that the Lord was moving above them into battle.*

Chapter VII: *Lost in thought and watching the convicts, the boy had not seen the guard.*

Chapter VII: *No one among them suddenly raised himself to the height of a man almost as tall as a cabin porch post.*

Chapter VIII: *The boy looked at the white-haired old man leaning over like he was listening for the plant to answer him.*

Chapter VII: *The teacher lit two lamps.*

Chapter VIII: *As the figure on the road drew near, it took shape and grew indistinct again in the wavering heat.*

Chapter VIII: *But he resolved he would not die, even with a half-dead body, because he wanted to come home again.*

Chapter VIII: *At the foot of one of the trees the boy's father sat, the lantern still burning by his side.*

Teacher Note: Choose an appropriate number of quotes for your students.

Conversations

Work in size-appropriate groups to write and perform the conversation that might have occurred in one of the following situations. If you prefer, you may use your own conversation idea for the characters in *Sounder.*

- The boy and the white-haired old man discuss the father's imprisonment. *(2 persons)*

- The boy's mother and father talk about the boy's education. *(2 persons)*

- The teacher and the boy's mother discuss her son's progress in school. *(2 persons)*

- When the boy grows up, he tells his son about Sounder. *(2 persons)*

- The sheriff and his deputies discuss going to arrest the boy's father. *(3 persons)*

- The boy's mother talks to the white landowner after her husband is arrested. *(2 persons)*

- The visiting preacher and the mayor discuss the sheriff's way of handling prisoners. *(2 persons)*

- The boy and his father discuss their feelings for Sounder. *(2 persons)*

- The boy tells his younger brother and sisters about what it is like to be in school. *(4 persons)*

- The boy grows up and tells his own son the story about David. *(2 persons)*

- The boy and his mother discuss the meanings of the songs she sings. *(2 persons)*

- The boy asks his father about what it was like to work on a chain gang. *(2 persons)*

- The old white-haired man and the boy discuss the Bill of Rights and the meaning of due process of law. *(2 persons)*

- The boy's mother goes to the store and overhears people talking about how her husband has been arrested. *(6 persons)*

- The younger children talk about how their older brother has changed since he started going to school. *(3 persons)*

- The boy's mother tells some other sharecroppers what happened to her husband. *(4 persons)*

Bibliography

Fiction

Armstrong, William H. *Sour Land.* (Harper & Row Junior Books Group, 1971)

Armstrong, William H. *Through Troubled Waters: A Young Father's Struggles with Grief.* (Abingdon, 1983)

Beatty, Patricia. *Turn Homeward.* (Morrow, 1984)

Greene, Bette. *Summer of My German Soldier.* (Bantam Books, 1984)

Hamilton, Virginia. *The People Could Fly: American Black Folktales.* (Alfred A. Knopf, 1988)

Highwater, Jamake. *Legend Days.* (Harper & Row Junior Books Group, 1984)

Houston, Jeanne W. and Houston, James D. *Farewell to Manzanar.* (Bantam, 1983)

Lee, Harper. *To Kill A Mockingbird.* (Warner Books, 1988)

Neufeld, John. *Edgar Allen.* (Signet Books, 1969)

Spinelli, Jerry. *Maniac McGee.* (Little, 1990)

Taylor, Mildred D. *The Friendship.* (Dial, 1987)

Taylor, Mildred D. *Mississippi Bridge.* (Dial, 1990)

Taylor, Mildred D. *Roll of Thunder, Hear My Cry.* (Bantam, 1984)

Taylor, Theodore. *The Cay.* (Doubleday, 1987)

Wisler, G. Clifton. *The Raid.* (Dutton, 1985)

Yates, Elizabeth. *Amos Fortune, Free Man.* (Penguin, 1989)

Yep, Laurence. *Dragonwings.* (Harper & Row Junior Books Group, 1977)

Nonfiction

Altman, Susan R. *Extraordinary Black Americans from Colonial to Contemporary Time.* (Childrens Press, 1988)

Cavanaugh, Arthur. *Bible Stories for Children.* (Macmillan, 1980)

Conrad, David E. *The Forgotten Farmers: The Story of Sharecroppers in the New Deal.* (Greenwood, 1965)

Davis, Ossie. *Escape to Freedom.* (Penguin, 1990)

Davis, Ronald. *Good & Faithful Labor: From Slavery to Sharecropping in the Natchez District.* 1860-1890. (Greenwood, 1982)

Ferris, Jeri. *Walking the Road to Freedom: A Story about Sojourner Truth.* (Carolrhoda Books, 1988)

Hamilton, Virginia. *Anthony Burns: The Defeat and Triumph of a Fugitive Slave.* (Knopf, 1988)

Hunt, P. *Bible Stories from the Old Testament.* (Putnam Publishing Group, 1987)

Kent, Zachary. *America the Beautiful, Georgia.* (Childrens Press, 1988)

Kester, Howard. *Revolt Among the Sharecroppers.* (Ayer, 1969)

Krass, Peter. Sojourner Truth. (Chelsea House, 1989)

McKissack, Pat. *Mary McLeod Bethune: A Great American Educator.* (Childrens Press, 1985)

McKissack, Pat. Sojourner Truth: *A Voice for Freedom.* (Enslow, 1992)

Petry, Ann. *Harriet Tubman: Conductor of the Underground Railway.* (Pocket Books, 1983)

Taylor, Roy G. *Sharecroppers: The Way We Really Were.* (J Mark, 1984)

Answer Key

Page 10

1. Accept appropriate responses.
2. Accept appropriate responses. Possible answers from the Author's Note include: the old black man sat in the balcony of the church away from the white people; no other black people ever came to the church. Possible answers from Chapter I include: a white man owned the land, but it was worked by Negro sharecroppers; there was a separate meeting house and school for the Negro sharecroppers; the white family lived in a big house while the boy and his family lived in a small cabin which belonged to the white landowner; the boy's mother did her family's wash as well as the white family's wash; the boy's parents could not read, but the adults in the white family could read.
3. The father was a sharecropper. In the winter, he would go hunting to be sure his family had enough to eat.
4. Sounder was a cross between a bulldog and Georgia redbone hound. He had great square jaws and head, a muscular neck, and a broad chest. His bark was so powerful it seemed to fill the air. He was a good hunter and could catch prey without breaking its skin.
5. Sounder got his name from the sound of his bark.
6. Sounder went hunting with the boy's father so that the family would have enough to eat.
7. The boy's mother laboriously picked the walnut meat out of the shells and sold them to the store. Then she would buy things that the family needed.
8. He felt safe and was not afraid.
9. There were sausages and a ham bone cooking on the stove. This was unusual because it was not a holiday or special occasion, and food was scarce in the winter.
10. The boy wanted to have a book to read with stories in it.

Page 15

1. Accept appropriate responses.
2. The boy's house smelled like ham bone for three days.
3. Three white men came to the boy's house. They were the sheriff and two deputies. They came to arrest the boy's father.
4. Calling the boy's father "boy" was an insult, indicating that he did not deserve any respect.
5. One of the white men shot Sounder when the dog started running, jumping, and barking at the wagon in which the father was being taken to jail.
6. The boy's mother thought Sounder would rather die alone.
7. The boy felt Sounder seemed more like a person and a member of the family than an animal.
8. The boy's mother went to the store to sell the walnut kernels. She also took what was left of the ham and pork sausage..
9. The boy found Sounder's ear. He put it in his pocket and slept with it under his pillow so that his wish to find Sounder alive would come true. In the morning, he decided to bury it with Sounder, but he lost it when he was looking for Sounder under the house.
10. The boy felt lonely, upset, and afraid.

Page 20

1. Accept appropriate responses.
2. The boy told the younger children not to ask for stick candy because she wouldn't have been able to afford any.
3. The boy's mother thought Sounder might have gone to the woods to get oak leaf acid on his wounds so they would heal.
4. The boy's mother brought fat meat, potatoes, a bottle of vanilla, and an empty cardboard box.
5. The mother felt like they were born to lose, and she was not sure that Sounder would come back.
6. The man said he searched the cake because it might have a steel file or a hacksaw blade in it. However, while he was searching the cake, he made a point to totally destroy it just to be mean.
7. On his way to town, the boy felt hopeful about meeting his father and happy to be taking the cake to him, but he also felt cold, hungry, afraid, and self-conscious. On his way home, the boy felt nothing but hate for the prison guard and pity for his father.
8. Suggested answers: The father probably did not want the boy exposed to that kind of humiliation and cruelty again; the father was ashamed to have the boy see him in jail.
9. The dog looked like a living skeleton. On the side where he was shot, his head and shoulder was reddish brown and hairless, his ear was just a stub, his eye was missing, and his front leg was useless. It seemed that he could only whine instead of bark.
10. The court ordered the boy's father to do hard labor.

Answer Key *(cont.)*

Page 23

Accept appropriate responses. Students should describe the following Amendments in their own words and tell why they are important.

First Amendment

Congress shall make no law respecting an establishment of religion, or prohibiting the free exercise thereof; or abridging the freedom of speech, or of the press; or the right of the people peaceably to assemble, and to petition the government for a redress of grievances.

Second Amendment

A well-regulated militia, being necessary to the security of a free State, the right of the people to keep and bear arms shall not be infringed.

Third Amendment

No soldier shall, in time of peace, be quartered in any house without the consent of the owner; nor in time of war but in a manner to be prescribed by law.

Fourth Amendment

The right of the people to be secure in their persons, houses, papers and effects, against unreasonable searches and seizures, shall not be violated, and no warrants shall issue but upon probable cause, supported by oath or affirmation, and particularly describing the place to be searched, and the persons or things to be seized.

Fifth Amendment

No person shall be held to answer for a capital or otherwise infamous crime, unless on a presentment or indictment of a grand jury, except in cases arising in the land or naval forces, or in the militia, when in actual service in time of war or public danger; nor shall any person be subject for the same offense to be twice put in jeopardy of life or limb; nor shall be compelled in any criminal case to be a witness against himself, nor be deprived of life, liberty, or property, without due process of law; nor shall private property be taken for public use, without just compensation.

Sixth Amendment

In all criminal prosecutions the accused shall enjoy the right to a speedy and public trial, by an impartial jury of the State and district wherein the crime shall have been committed, which district shall have been previously ascertained by law, and to be informed of the nature and cause of the accusation; to be confronted with the witnesses against him; to have compulsory process for obtaining witnesses in his favor, and to have the assistance of counsel for his defense.

Seventh Amendment

In suits of common law, where the value in controversy shall exceed twenty dollars, the right of trial by jury shall be preserved, and no fact tried by a jury shall be otherwise reexamined in any court of the United States than according to the rules of the common law.

Eighth Amendment

Excessive bail shall not be required, nor excessive fines imposed, nor cruel and unusual punishments inflicted.

Ninth Amendment

The enumeration in the Constitution of certain rights shall not be construed to deny or disparage others retained by the people.

Tenth Amendment

The powers not delegated to the United States by the Constitution, nor prohibited by it to the States, are reserved to the States respectively, or to the people.

Page 25

1. Accept appropriate responses.

2. The boy worked in the fields and did yard work at the big houses in the spring.

3. The boy wanted to find his father.

4. The boy found that people threw newspapers and magazines into the trash barrels. He thought they were wonderful because he could use them to practice his reading.

5. The boy listened to the wind because it reminded him of the story his mother had told him about King David. In the story, David knew the Lord was on his side and would help him win when he heard the wind moving in the tops of the cedar trees.

6. The father has been on the chain gang several years.

7. A prison guard smashed the boy's hand on the fence when he was standing at the fence, trying to determine if one of the convicts on the chain gang was his father.

8. The boy knew that if his father had been there he would have jumped up and grabbed the guard by the neck for hurting his son.

9. The boy tried to read it and took it with him.

Answer Key *(cont.)*

10. The boy was amazed that the old teacher had two lamps burning in the same room, one stove for cooking and one stove for warming the room, and shelves filled with books.

Page 30

1. Accept appropriate responses.
2. The boy told his mother and the children about the old teacher. He told them because he had been asked to live with the teacher.
3. The mother thought that it was meant to be because she believed it was a sign from God that the boy met the teacher.
4. The boy went to school during the school year, and he worked in the fields at home during the summer.
5. Six years had passed since the father was taken away, because six crops of persimmons and wild grapes had ripened.
6. The mother thought the "dog days" of summer were so hot that dogs went mad.
7. Sounder suddenly barked when he recognized the person who was walking down the road.
8. The father was walking down the road.
9. The father was partially paralyzed because half of his body has been crushed during a dynamite blast in the prison quarry.
10. Accept responses which indicate an understanding that something is never completely dead as long as there is someone living who remembers it.

Page 33

Page 38-41

Create a display of these culminating activities for the bulletin board or shelf.

Page 42

Matching

1. the boy
2. the deputy
3. the mother
4. the father
5. the teacher

True or False

1. False
2. True
3. True
4. False
5. True

Short Answers

1. The father was a sharecropper.
2. The mother thought Sounder was drawing the poison out of his wound with oak-leaf acid.
3. The guard said the cake might have a steel file or a hacksaw in it, but he also did it to be cruel.
4. The teacher the boy met while looking for his father asked the boy to live with him and go to school.
5. Sounder loved his master and probably missed him so much that he did not feel like barking.

Essay

1. Accept appropriate responses.
2. Accept appropriate responses.

Page 43

Accept all reasonable and well-supported answers.

Page 44

Perform the conversations in class. Ask students to respond to the conversations in several different ways, such as, "Are the conversations realistic?" or, "Are the words the characters say in line with their personalities?"